Democracy Innovation

Politics By The People

Caroline Reni Johnson

Table of contents

Introduction: The Importance of Democracy

Democracy is a system of government that allows citizens to participate in decision-making processes, either directly or through elected representatives. It is a fundamental aspect of modern society and plays a crucial role in shaping the lives of individuals and communities. The importance of democracy cannot be overstated, as it ensures the protection of individual rights, promotes equality, fosters economic development, and encourages political stability.

Firstly, democracy guarantees the protection of individual rights and freedoms. In a democratic society, citizens have the right to express their opinions, assemble peacefully, and engage in political activities without fear of persecution. This freedom allows for the development of diverse perspectives and encourages open dialogue and debate. Additionally, democratic systems provide mechanisms for citizens to hold their leaders accountable through regular elections and the rule of law. This ensures that those in power are responsive to the needs and aspirations of the people they represent.

CANADA
NORTH
AMERICA
Salt Lake City
San Francisco
UNITED STATES OF
AMERICA
Los Angeles
Hermosi
N
W E
S
U.S.A.)
Direction of the
Earth's Rotation
Kiribati 135° EQUATOR
120°
Christmas I)
SO
PA
O
POLITICS

Secondly, democracy promotes equality among citizens. By granting everyone an equal voice in decision-making processes, regardless of their social status or background, democracy ensures that no one group dominates or marginalizes others. It provides opportunities for marginalized groups to have their concerns addressed and their interests represented. This inclusivity fosters social cohesion and reduces social tensions, creating a more harmonious and equitable society.

Furthermore, democracy is closely linked to economic development. Studies have shown that countries with democratic systems tend to experience higher levels of economic growth and prosperity. This is because democracy encourages transparency, accountability, and the rule of law – all essential elements for attracting investment and fostering entrepreneurship. Moreover, democratic societies are more likely to prioritize education, healthcare, infrastructure development, and social welfare programs that contribute to overall economic progress.

In addition to these benefits, democracy also plays a vital role in ensuring political stability. By providing avenues for peaceful resolution of conflicts and power transitions through elections, democratic systems reduce the likelihood of violence or civil unrest. They allow for peaceful transitions of power when leaders fail to meet the expectations of the people, preventing the consolidation of power in the hands of a few and reducing the risk of authoritarianism or dictatorship.

Furthermore, democracy encourages active citizen participation and engagement in public affairs. It empowers individuals to have a say in decisions that affect their lives, fostering a sense of ownership and responsibility towards their communities and nation. This engagement can lead to increased civic awareness, political education, and a more informed electorate. In turn, this strengthens democratic institutions and ensures that government policies reflect the will of the people

Democracy is of utmost importance for a just and prosperous society. It protects individual rights, promotes equality, fosters economic development, ensures political stability, and encourages citizen participation.

Other Books from the publisher

https://mybook.to/Grow_your_mind
https://mybook.to/TravelAdventure
https://mybook.to/WinterApple
https://mybook.to/Teenage_Sexuality
https://mybook.to/love_language

Chapter 1: Historical Background: **Origins** of Democracy

Democracy actually has a long and fascinating historical background. It all started in ancient Greece, around the 5th century BCE. The city-state of Athens is often credited as the birthplace of democracy.

In Athens, the people had a direct say in decision-making through a system called "direct democracy." Citizens would gather in an assembly, where they could debate and vote on various issues. This was a significant shift from the previous system of rule by a few powerful individuals.

The concept of democracy in Athens was influenced by the ideas of philosophers like Plato and Aristotle. They believed that power should lie with the people, as they were the ones affected by the decisions made by the government.

Over time, the idea of democracy spread to other city-states in Greece. However, it's important to note that not everyone was considered a citizen in ancient Athens. Women, slaves, and foreigners were excluded from participating in the democratic process.

Fast forward to the modern era, and democracy has evolved significantly. Different forms of democracy have emerged in various countries around the world. Representative democracy, where citizens elect representatives to make decisions on their behalf, is the most common form today.

Democracy has been a powerful force for change and progress throughout history. It has provided a platform for people to voice their opinions, protect their rights, and hold their leaders accountable. Of course, no system is perfect, and democracies face their own challenges and complexities.

It's fascinating to see how the concept of democracy has evolved and shaped the world we live in today. So many countries now embrace democratic principles and strive to create inclusive and participatory societies. It's definitely a topic worth exploring further if you're interested in politics and history.

As mentioned earlier, ancient Greece, particularly Athens, played a pivotal role in the origins of democracy. The Athenian democracy was unique for its direct participation of citizens in decision-making. The assembly, known as the Ekklesia, was open to all male citizens over the age of 18. They would gather on a hill called the Pnyx to discuss and vote on matters of importance to the city-state.

One of the key figures associated with the development of democracy in Athens was Cleisthenes. In 508 BCE, he introduced a series of reforms that aimed to empower the common citizens and reduce the influence of aristocratic families. These reforms included the creation of demes, which were local administrative units, and the introduction of ostracism, a process to exile individuals deemed a threat to the democracy.

The democratic system in Athens faced its fair share of challenges. The Peloponnesian War, which lasted from 431 to 404 BCE, put a strain on the democratic institutions. The war weakened Athens and led to a loss of confidence in the democratic system, eventually leading to the rise of Macedonian rule under Alexander the Great.

After the decline of Greek democracy, the concept of democracy largely disappeared from the political landscape for centuries. It wasn't until the Enlightenment period in the 17th and 18th centuries that the idea of democracy began to resurface. Thinkers like John Locke and Jean-Jacques Rousseau advocated for the sovereignty of the people and the importance of consent in governance.

The American and French Revolutions in the late 18th century further propelled the development of democratic ideals. The United States, with its Constitution and Bill of Rights, established a representative democracy that became a model for many nations. The French Revolution, with its cry of "Liberty, Equality, Fraternity," also sought to establish a democratic system.

Since then, democracy has continued to evolve and spread across the globe. Different countries have adopted their own variations of democracy, incorporating elements of direct participation, representative government, and the protection of individual rights. Today, democracy is considered a fundamental value in many societies and is upheld as a standard for good governance.

It's truly fascinating to see how the concept of democracy has endured and adapted throughout history. The struggles and triumphs of the past have shaped the democratic systems we have today. Understanding this historical background helps us appreciate the importance of democracy and the ongoing efforts to strengthen and protect.

Did you know that the word "democracy" comes from the Greek words "demos" (meaning "people") and "kratos" (meaning "rule" or "power")? So, democracy literally means "rule by the people." Pretty cool, right?

Now, let's take a closer look at the different types of democracy that exist today. One common form is representative democracy, where citizens elect representatives to make decisions on their behalf. This is the system we see in many countries, like the United States, where people vote for their president, senators, and members of Congress.

Another type is direct democracy, which harkens back to the ancient Greek model. In direct democracy, citizens have a direct say in the decision-making process. This can be done through referendums or town hall meetings, where people come together to discuss and vote on important issues.

There are also hybrid forms of democracy that combine elements of both representative and direct democracy. For example, some countries have citizen initiatives, where citizens can propose laws and gather signatures to put them on the ballot for a direct vote.

Of course, democracy is not without its challenges. It requires an informed and engaged citizenry, as well as mechanisms to protect minority rights and ensure fair representation. It's an ongoing process that requires constant vigilance and participation from all of us.

But at its core, democracy is a beautiful concept that gives power to the people and allows for diverse voices to be heard. It's about fostering dialogue, respecting different perspectives, and working together to create a better society.

Chapter 2: Democratic Principles: Equality and Freedom

These two principles are at the heart of democracy and play a crucial role in shaping our societies. These principles are the pillars of a democratic society, ensuring fairness, justice, and the protection of individual rights.
So, let's explore them in detail

1. Equality: In a democratic society, equality means that all individuals are treated with fairness and have equal opportunities. It means that no one should be discriminated against based on their race, gender, religion, or any other characteristic. Equality ensures that everyone has an equal chance to succeed and thrive.

2. Political Equality: Democratic principles uphold the idea of political equality, which means that every citizen has an equal right to participate in the political process. This includes the right to vote, run for office, and express opinions freely. Political equality ensures that each person's voice carries the same weight in decision-making.

3. Social Equality: Democracy also aims for social equality, which means that all members of society have access to the same rights, resources, and opportunities. It seeks to bridge the gaps between different social classes and promote a more equitable distribution of wealth and resources.

4. Economic Equality: In a democratic society, economic equality strives to reduce disparities in income and wealth. It means ensuring that everyone has access to basic necessities, education, healthcare, and economic opportunities. Economic equality helps to prevent the concentration of power and resources in the hands of a few.

5. Freedom: Freedom is another fundamental principle of democracy. It encompasses both personal and political freedoms. Let's explore them further:

6. Personal Freedom: Personal freedom refers to the individual's right to make choices, express themselves, and live their lives without undue interference. It includes freedom of speech, religion, assembly, and the right

to privacy. Personal freedom allows individuals to pursue their own happiness and live according to their values.

7. Political Freedom: Political freedom is the freedom to participate in the political process, express political opinions, and choose representatives. It includes the right to criticize the government, form political parties, and engage in peaceful protests. Political freedom ensures that citizens have a say in shaping the policies that affect their lives.

8. Rule of Law: Democracy is built on the principle of the rule of law, which means that all individuals, including government officials, are subject to the same laws and regulations. The rule of law ensures that no one is above the law and that justice is applied equally to all.

9. Protection of Minority Rights: Democracy places a strong emphasis on protecting the rights of minorities. It recognizes that the majority should not be able

10. Equality: In a democratic system, equality means that every person is treated with fairness and has equal opportunities. It goes beyond just legal equality and aims to address social and economic disparities. It ensures that individuals are not discriminated against based on their race, gender, religion, or any other characteristic. Equality in a democracy means that everyone has a voice and an equal chance to succeed.

11. Political Equality: One of the key aspects of democracy is political equality. It means that every citizen has an equal right to participate in the political process. This includes the right to vote, run for office, and have their voice heard. Political equality ensures that decisions are made by the people and that no one group dominates the political landscape.

12. Social Equality: Democracy also strives for social equality. It aims to create a society where everyone has access to the same rights, resources, and opportunities. This means bridging the gaps between different social classes and ensuring that basic needs such as education, healthcare, and housing are available to all. Social equality promotes a more inclusive and cohesive society.

13. Economic Equality: In a democratic society, economic equality is an important principle. It seeks to reduce disparities in income and wealth and ensure that everyone has a fair chance to succeed economically. This means providing equal opportunities for education, job prospects, and upward mobility. Economic equality helps prevent the concentration of power and resources in the hands of a few.

14. Freedom: Freedom is a fundamental principle of democracy, encompassing personal and political freedoms.

15. Personal Freedom: Personal freedom means that individuals have the right to make choices, express themselves, and live their lives without undue interference. It includes freedom of speech, religion, assembly, and the right to privacy. Personal freedom allows individuals to pursue their own happiness and live according to their values.

16. Political Freedom: Political freedom is the freedom to participate in the political process, voice political opinions, and choose representatives. It includes the right to criticize the government, form political parties, and engage in peaceful protests. Political freedom ensures that citizens have a say in shaping the policies that affect their lives.

17. Rule of Law: Democracy is built on the principle of the rule of law. This means that all individuals, including government officials, are subject to the same laws and regulations.

Chapter 3: Forms of Democracy: Direct vs. Representative

There are different forms of democracy: direct democracy and representative democracy, here is a quick break down.

Direct Democracy

In a direct democracy, citizens have a direct role in decision-making and policy formulation. This means that individuals participate directly in the political process, rather than relying on elected representatives. Direct democracy allows citizens to vote on specific issues, laws, or policies through referendums, initiatives, or town hall meetings.

Direct democracy is a form of democracy where citizens have a direct say in decision-making. It's like being part of a big group chat where everyone gets to vote on important issues. In direct democracy, citizens can participate in decision-making through methods like referendums, where they directly vote on specific laws or policies. This allows people to have a direct influence on the laws that affect them.

One of the benefits of direct democracy is that it gives individuals a strong sense of involvement and empowerment. It's like having a voice and being heard in the decision-making process. Direct democracy also promotes transparency and accountability because decisions are made collectively by the people. It's like having a say in what goes on in your community or country.

However, direct democracy also comes with its challenges. It can be time-consuming and logistically difficult to involve every citizen in decision-making. Imagine trying to get everyone in a group chat to agree on something! Additionally, not everyone may have the necessary knowledge or expertise to make informed decisions on complex issues. It's like trying to discuss rocket science with your friends who aren't into that stuff.

On the other hand, we have representative democracy, which is like electing someone to speak on your behalf in that big group chat. In representative democracy, citizens elect representatives who make decisions and pass laws on their behalf. These representatives are like the voice of the people in the decision-making process.

Benefits of Direct Democracy: One of the main benefits of direct democracy is that it gives citizens a direct voice in shaping policies and laws. It promotes active citizen engagement and ensures that decisions are made in the best interest of the people. Direct democracy also fosters a sense of responsibility and accountability among citizens, as they are directly involved in the decision-making process.

Challenges of Direct Democracy: However, direct democracy also poses challenges. It can be time-consuming and resource-intensive to involve all citizens in decision-making. Direct democracy may not be feasible for large populations, as it requires extensive organization and coordination. Additionally, citizens may not always have the necessary expertise or information to make informed decisions on complex issues.

Representative Democracy

In a representative democracy, citizens elect representatives to make decisions on their behalf. These elected officials, such as members of parliament or congress, are responsible for representing the interests and concerns of their constituents. Representative democracy allows for more efficient decision-making and governance, as elected representatives have the time, resources, and expertise to delve into complex issues.

Representative democracy offers some advantages. Elected representatives have the time and resources to study and understand complex issues. They can dedicate their efforts to making informed decisions that benefit the people they represent. It's like having a friend who's really good at researching and analyzing stuff, and you trust them to make decisions on your behalf.

However, representative democracy also has its challenges. There is always the risk of elected officials becoming disconnected from the needs and concerns of the people. It's like when your friend starts making decisions without considering what you actually want. There can also be concerns about the influence of money and special interests in the electoral process, which can undermine the principle of equal representation.

To find a balance between direct and representative democracy, some countries use a hybrid system. It's like having different group chats for different topics. They may have direct democracy elements, like referendums, for certain issues, while still relying on elected representatives for overall governance.

So, in a nutshell, direct democracy is like being part of a big group chat where everyone gets to vote.

Benefits of Representative Democracy: Representative democracy offers several advantages. It allows for the representation of diverse perspectives and interests in the decision-making process. Elected representatives can dedicate their time and efforts to studying policies, debating issues, and making informed decisions on behalf of the people. Representative democracy also provides stability and continuity in governance, as elected officials serve for a fixed term.

Challenges of Representative Democracy: However, representative democracy is not without its challenges. There is always the risk of elected officials becoming disconnected from the needs and desires of their constituents. This can lead to a sense of alienation or distrust among citizens. Additionally, there may be concerns about the influence of money and special interests in the electoral process, potentially undermining the democratic ideals of equal representation.

Hybrid Systems

Many modern democracies employ a combination of direct and representative democracy. This hybrid approach seeks to strike a balance between citizen participation and efficient decision-making. For example, some countries use referendums or citizen initiatives for specific issues, while still relying on elected representatives for overall governance.

Chapter 4: The Role of Political Parties

Political parties play a crucial role in any democratic system. They serve as the primary means through which citizens can participate in the political process, voice their opinions, and influence government policies. The role of political parties encompasses various aspects, including representation, mobilization, policy formulation, and accountability.

Firstly, political parties provide a platform for citizens to express their interests and concerns. By organizing individuals with similar ideologies and goals, parties act as intermediaries between the government and the people. They articulate the needs of different sections of society and present them to policymakers. This representation is essential for ensuring that diverse voices are heard and considered in the decision-making process.

Secondly, political parties play a vital role in mobilizing voters during elections. They help educate citizens about political issues, candidates, and party platforms. Parties engage in grassroots activities such as door-to-door campaigning, organizing rallies, and conducting voter registration drives. These efforts not only increase voter turnout but also foster civic engagement and participation.

Furthermore, political parties contribute to policy formulation by developing comprehensive platforms that outline their stance on various issues. Through internal debates and discussions, parties establish their policy priorities and propose solutions to societal challenges. These platforms provide voters with a clear understanding of what each party stands for and helps them make informed choices during elections.

Political parties also facilitate governance by serving as a mechanism for political recruitment. They identify potential leaders who can represent their values and aspirations effectively. Parties groom these individuals through internal party structures, providing them with opportunities to gain experience and develop leadership skills. This process ensures a steady supply of capable politicians who can assume positions of power and responsibility.

In addition to representation and governance, political parties promote accountability within the political system. Parties act as watchdogs by monitoring the actions of elected officials from other parties. They scrutinize government policies, hold officials accountable for their actions or lack thereof, and highlight any instances of corruption or malfeasance. This oversight function is crucial for maintaining transparency and integrity in the political process.

Moreover, political parties serve as a platform for fostering political stability and consensus-building. In multi-party systems, parties often form coalitions to gain a majority in the legislature and form a government. These coalitions require negotiation and compromise, encouraging parties to find common ground and work together towards shared objectives. This collaborative approach promotes stability and prevents extreme ideologies from dominating the political landscape.

Political parties also contribute to the development of democratic institutions. They help establish rules and procedures for elections, ensuring that they are free, fair, and transparent. Parties play a crucial role in monitoring electoral processes, preventing fraud, and promoting democratic values such as respect for human rights and the rule of law.

Furthermore, political parties facilitate public debate by providing platforms for discussion and dialogue. They organize debates, town hall meetings, and public forums where citizens can engage with politicians and express their opinions. These interactions foster an informed electorate and encourage the exchange of ideas necessary for a vibrant democracy.

Additionally, political parties act as channels for policy implementation. When elected to power, parties have the responsibility to translate their promises into action. They formulate legislation, develop budgets, and implement policies that align with their party platforms. Through this process, parties are accountable not only to their supporters but also to the broader public.

Political parties also contribute to social cohesion by representing diverse interests within society. They bring together individuals from different backgrounds, ethnicities, religions, and socioeconomic classes under a common ideological umbrella. By fostering inclusivity and providing a platform for marginalized groups to voice their concerns, parties promote social integration and reduce societal divisions.

Political parties play a crucial role in democracy as they serve as the backbone of the political system. They are essential for the functioning and stability of democratic governments. Here are ten paragraphs explaining the importance of political parties in democracy:

1. Representation: Political parties provide a platform for citizens to express their political views and interests. They act as intermediaries between the government and the people, representing various social, economic, and ideological groups within society. Through parties, individuals can join forces with like-minded individuals to collectively advocate for their concerns.

2. Formation of Government: In a democracy, political parties compete in elections to form governments. Parties present their policies and visions to voters, who then choose the party that aligns with their values and goals. The winning party or coalition forms the government, ensuring that power is transferred peacefully and democratically.

3. Accountability: Political parties hold elected officials accountable for their actions. They monitor government performance, criticize policies they disagree with, and propose alternative solutions. By doing so, parties ensure that elected representatives remain responsive to the needs and aspirations of the people.

4. Policy Development: Political parties are responsible for developing policies that address societal challenges and meet public demands. Parties debate issues, conduct research, consult experts, and engage with citizens to formulate comprehensive policy platforms. These policies guide decision-making when parties come into power.

5. Representation of Diverse Interests: Democracy is characterized by diversity, with multiple interest groups vying for influence. Political parties act as vehicles for aggregating these diverse interests into coherent policy agendas. They help bridge societal divisions by accommodating different perspectives and finding common ground through compromise.

6. Participation and Mobilization: Political parties encourage citizen participation in politics by providing opportunities for individuals to get involved in campaigns, volunteer activities, and grassroots movements. Parties mobilize supporters through rallies, door-to-door canvassing, and other forms of outreach, fostering civic engagement and strengthening democratic participation.

7. Stability and Governance: Political parties contribute to political stability by providing a structured framework for governance. They establish rules, procedures, and norms that guide the functioning of governments. Parties help maintain order and continuity by facilitating the peaceful transfer of power through elections.

8. Education and Awareness: Political parties play an educational role in democracy. They inform citizens about political issues, policies, and candidates through their campaigns, manifestos, and public debates. Parties help raise awareness among voters, empowering them to make informed decisions during elections.

9. Representation of Marginalized Groups: Political parties can serve as platforms for marginalized groups to have their voices heard and interests represented. Parties that champion social justice, gender equality, minority rights, or environmental sustainability can provide a platform for underrepresented communities to advocate for their concerns within the political system.

10. International Relations: Political parties also play a role in international relations. They form alliances with like-minded parties in other countries, fostering diplomatic relations and promoting cooperation on global issues. Parties can influence foreign policy decisions and contribute to shaping international agreements and treaties.

Political parties are essential for the functioning of democracy as they represent diverse interests, develop policies, hold governments accountable, mobilize citizens, and ensure stability in governance. They provide a platform for citizen participation, educate voters, represent marginalized groups, and contribute to international relations. Without political parties, democracy would lack the necessary structure and mechanisms to effectively govern societies based on the will of the people.

Lastly, political parties play a critical role in shaping public opinion through their communication strategies. Parties use various media channels to disseminate information about their policies, achievements, and criticisms of opponents. This communication helps shape public discourse and influences public opinion on important issues.

Other books from the publisher

https://mybook.to/Grow_your_mind
https://mybook.to/TravelAdventure
https://mybook.to/WinterApple
https://mybook.to/Teenage_Sexuality
https://mybook.to/love_language

Chapter 5: Elections and Voting Systems

Elections and voting systems are fundamental components of a democracy. They play a crucial role in ensuring that citizens have the opportunity to participate in the decision-making process and choose their representatives. In this extensive discussion, we will explore the importance of elections, different types of voting systems, and their impact on democracy.

Firstly, elections provide citizens with the power to elect their leaders. Through the act of voting, individuals can express their preferences and select candidates who they believe will best represent their interests. This process ensures that political power is not concentrated in the hands of a few but distributed among the people.

Moreover, elections foster accountability in a democratic system. By holding regular elections, citizens have the ability to evaluate the performance of their elected officials and decide whether they should be reelected or replaced. This mechanism encourages politicians to act in the best interest of their constituents, as they know they will be held accountable for their actions at the ballot box.

Elections and voting systems are crucial components of democratic societies. They provide citizens with the opportunity to participate in the decision-making process and choose their representatives. This process ensures that power is distributed among the people and prevents authoritarian rule.

One key aspect of elections is the concept of universal suffrage, which means that all eligible citizens have the right to vote. This principle promotes equality and inclusivity, as it allows every individual to have a say in shaping their government. Universal suffrage has evolved over time, with many countries expanding voting rights to include previously marginalized groups such as women, racial minorities, and young people.

Voting systems play a significant role in determining how elections are conducted and how votes are translated into seats or positions of power. There are various types of voting systems used around the world, each with its own advantages and disadvantages.

One commonly used system is the plurality or first-past-the-post system. In this system, voters cast their ballots for a single candidate, and the candidate with the most votes wins. While this system is simple and easy to understand, critics argue that it can lead to a lack of representation for minority groups since candidates who receive a plurality of votes may not necessarily have majority support.

VOTE

Another widely used system is proportional representation (PR). PR aims to ensure that the number of seats a party receives in an election corresponds closely to its share of the popular vote. This system allows for greater representation of diverse political views and encourages coalition-building among parties. However, PR can also result in more fragmented legislatures and potentially slower decision-making processes.

Some countries use a mixed-member proportional (MMP) system, which combines elements of both plurality and proportional representation. Under this system, voters cast two ballots - one for a candidate in their constituency and another for a political party. The constituency seats are determined by plurality voting, while additional seats are allocated to parties based on their overall share of the vote.

Other voting systems include ranked-choice voting, where voters rank candidates in order of preference, and the single transferable vote, which allows voters to rank candidates and transfer their votes if their preferred candidate is eliminated.

The choice of voting system can have significant implications for the representation and functioning of a democracy. It can impact the number of political parties, the level of voter turnout, and the overall stability of the government. Therefore, it is crucial for countries to carefully consider the strengths and weaknesses of different voting systems before implementing them.

In recent years, there has been increased interest in electoral reform and exploring alternative voting systems. This is driven by a desire to address issues such as voter apathy, political polarization, and underrepresentation. Some proposed reforms include adopting proportional representation systems, introducing mandatory voting laws, or implementing online voting to increase accessibility.

However, changing voting systems is not without challenges. It requires careful planning, public consultation, and often constitutional amendments. Moreover, any changes must be accompanied by robust education campaigns to ensure that citizens understand how the new system works and are able to make informed choices.

Overall, elections and voting systems are essential components of democratic governance. They provide citizens with a voice in shaping their government and hold elected officials accountable. The choice of a voting system should be based on principles of fairness, inclusivity, and effectiveness in representing diverse voices within society.

There are various types of voting systems used in democracies around the world. One common system is plurality or first-past-the-post (FPTP), where voters choose one candidate, and the candidate with the most votes wins. While this system is simple and easy to understand, critics argue that it often leads to a lack of proportional representation and can result in a two-party dominance.

Another widely used system is proportional representation (PR), which aims to allocate seats in proportion to each party's share of the vote. PR allows for greater representation of minority parties and can lead to more diverse legislatures. However, it can also result in fragmented governments and coalition-building challenges.

Ranked-choice voting (RCV) is gaining popularity as an alternative system. In RCV, voters rank candidates in order of preference. If no candidate receives a majority in the first round, lower-ranked candidates are eliminated until one candidate reaches a majority. This system encourages candidates to appeal to a broader base of support and reduces the need for strategic voting.

The choice of voting system has significant implications for democracy. It can influence the representation of different groups, the competitiveness of elections, and the overall legitimacy of the political system. Therefore, it is essential to carefully consider the strengths and weaknesses of each system when designing electoral processes.

In addition to the voting system itself, other factors such as campaign financing, voter registration, and access to polling stations can impact the fairness and inclusivity of elections. Ensuring that all citizens have equal opportunities to participate in the electoral process is crucial for a healthy democracy.

Furthermore, elections are not just about choosing representatives; they also provide a platform for public debate and discussion. Election campaigns allow candidates to present their policies and engage with voters on important issues. This exchange of ideas helps to shape public opinion and encourages citizens to become more informed about political matters.

However, elections are not without challenges. Voter apathy and low turnout rates are persistent concerns in many democracies. Efforts must be made to engage citizens, particularly marginalized groups, and encourage their participation in the electoral process. Education campaigns, voter outreach programs, and improved accessibility can help address these issues.

Moreover, elections can be vulnerable to manipulation and fraud. Safeguards such as independent election commissions, transparent ballot counting processes, and robust oversight mechanisms are necessary to ensure free and fair elections. International observers can also play a crucial role in monitoring elections and providing an impartial assessment of their integrity.

It is important to recognize that elections alone do not guarantee a fully functioning democracy. They are just one aspect of a broader democratic system that includes respect for human rights, rule of law, freedom of speech, and an independent judiciary. These elements work together to create an environment where citizens can freely express their opinions and hold their leaders accountable.

Chapter 6: The Power of the People: Participatory Democracy

Participatory democracy is a form of government where citizens actively participate in decision-making processes and have a direct influence on policy-making. It empowers individuals by giving them a voice and allowing them to shape the direction of their communities and societies. This form of democracy is based on the belief that the power lies with the people, and it is their active involvement that drives progress and ensures accountability.

One of the key benefits of participatory democracy is that it fosters a sense of ownership and responsibility among citizens. When people are directly involved in decision-making, they feel more invested in the outcomes and are more likely to actively contribute to the betterment of their communities. This leads to increased civic engagement and a stronger sense of community cohesion.

Participatory democracy also promotes transparency and accountability. When decisions are made collectively, there is greater scrutiny and oversight, as citizens can hold their representatives accountable for their actions. This helps prevent corruption and ensures that decisions are made in the best interest of the public rather than for personal gain.

Furthermore, participatory democracy allows for diverse perspectives to be heard and considered. By involving a wide range of stakeholders in decision-making processes, different viewpoints can be taken into account, leading to more comprehensive and inclusive policies. This helps avoid marginalization and discrimination, as decisions are made with a broader understanding of the needs and concerns of all members of society.

Another advantage of participatory democracy is its potential to address social inequalities. By giving marginalized groups a platform to voice their concerns, participatory democracy can help bridge gaps in representation and empower those who have historically been excluded from decision-making processes. This can lead to more equitable policies that address systemic injustices.

Participatory democracy also encourages active citizenship by fostering a culture of civic education and engagement. When citizens are actively involved in decision-making processes, they become more informed about political issues and develop a deeper understanding of how government works. This leads to an empowered citizenry that is more likely to participate in other aspects of civic life, such as voting, volunteering, and advocating for social change.

Moreover, participatory democracy can enhance the quality of decision-making. When decisions are made collectively, they benefit from the collective wisdom and expertise of a diverse group of individuals. This can lead to more informed and well-rounded decisions that take into account a broader range of perspectives and potential consequences.

Participatory democracy also promotes innovation and creativity. By involving citizens in decision-making processes, new ideas and solutions can emerge from unexpected sources. This can lead to innovative approaches to societal challenges and foster a culture of continuous improvement.

Furthermore, participatory democracy strengthens trust between citizens and their government. When people feel that their voices are heard and their opinions matter, they are more likely to have faith in the democratic process and the institutions that govern them. This can help build a more stable and harmonious society.

However, participatory democracy also has its challenges. It requires active citizen engagement, which can be difficult to achieve in societies with low levels of political awareness or apathy. It also requires resources and infrastructure to facilitate citizen participation, such as public forums, online platforms, and education programs.

Participatory democracy is a powerful tool for empowering citizens and ensuring accountability in governance. It promotes transparency, inclusivity, social justice, active citizenship, quality decision-making, innovation, trust, and civic engagement. While it may face challenges in implementation, its benefits far outweigh the obstacles. By harnessing the power of the people through participatory democracy, societies can create more just and inclusive systems of governance that truly represent the interests of all citizens.

Participatory democracy Is all about the power of the people and how everyone can actively participate in decision-making. It's like being at a party where everyone gets to have a say and shape the direction of their community or country.

Participatory democracy is a form of democracy where citizens are directly involved in the decision-making process. It goes beyond just voting for representatives; it emphasizes active participation and engagement from the people. It's like being part of a lively conversation where everyone's ideas and opinions are valued.

In participatory democracy, citizens have the opportunity to directly influence policies, laws, and public affairs. There are various ways in which this can happen. For example, citizens can participate in town hall meetings, public forums, or community assemblies where they can voice their concerns, propose ideas, and engage in discussions. It's like having a platform to express your thoughts and contribute to the decision-making process.

Another aspect of participatory democracy is citizen initiatives and referendums. This means that citizens can propose and vote on specific issues or policies directly. It's like having the power to bring up topics for discussion and make decisions collectively. This way, decisions are not solely in the hands of elected representatives, but in the hands of the people themselves.

Participatory democracy promotes inclusivity and diversity. It ensures that everyone's voice is heard, regardless of their background or social status. It's like having a party where everyone is invited and everyone's opinions matter. This helps to foster a sense of ownership and responsibility among citizens, as they feel more connected to the decisions that affect their lives.

One of the great advantages of participatory democracy is that it encourages active citizenship. It motivates people to become more informed about public affairs, engage in dialogue, and take action. It's like being part of a movement where everyone is working together towards a common goal. This can lead to a more vibrant and dynamic democracy, where people feel empowered and invested in the well-being of their community.

However, it's important to acknowledge that participatory democracy also has its challenges. It can be time-consuming and require a lot of effort to ensure that everyone's voices are heard and considered. It's like organizing a big party and making sure that everyone has a chance to speak. Additionally, there may be logistical challenges in terms of coordinating and implementing decisions made through participatory processes.

Despite these challenges, participatory democracy offers a valuable alternative to traditional forms of democracy.

Chapter 7: Media and Democracy: The Fourth Estate

The concept of the Fourth Estate refers to the media's role as a crucial pillar of democracy. It represents the idea that the media acts as a check on the three branches of government, ensuring transparency, accountability, and serving as a voice for the people. In modern society, the media plays a vital role in shaping public opinion, disseminating information, and holding those in power accountable.

One of the fundamental principles of democracy is an informed citizenry. The media serves as a conduit for information, providing citizens with access to news and analysis on a wide range of topics. Through investigative journalism, the media uncovers corruption, exposes wrongdoing, and sheds light on issues that might otherwise remain hidden from public view. This function is essential for maintaining an open and transparent society.

Furthermore, the media acts as a watchdog over government institutions and officials. By reporting on political activities, policy decisions, and electoral processes, it ensures that those in power are held accountable for their actions. Through critical analysis and fact-checking, journalists play a crucial role in challenging misinformation and propaganda, helping citizens make informed decisions.

The media also serves as a platform for diverse voices and perspectives. In a democratic society, it is essential to have access to different viewpoints to foster debate and dialogue. The Fourth Estate provides space for marginalized communities, opposition parties, activists, and ordinary citizens to express their opinions and concerns. This diversity of voices strengthens democracy by ensuring that no single narrative dominates public discourse.

Moreover, the media acts as a bridge between citizens and policymakers. It provides a platform for citizens to voice their concerns and grievances while also facilitating communication between elected officials and their constituents. Through interviews, debates, town halls, and other forms of engagement, the media enables dialogue between different stakeholders in society.

In addition to its role in informing citizens and holding power accountable, the media also plays a significant role during elections. It provides coverage of campaigns, candidates' platforms, and electoral processes, allowing voters to make informed choices. By monitoring campaign financing, fact-checking political statements, and organizing debates, the media ensures that elections are fair and transparent.

However, the media's role as the Fourth Estate is not without challenges. The rise of social media and digital platforms has led to an explosion of information sources, making it increasingly difficult for citizens to discern reliable news from misinformation or fake news. This challenge highlights the importance of media literacy and critical thinking skills in today's society.

Another challenge is the concentration of media ownership in the hands of a few powerful corporations or individuals. This concentration can limit diversity of voices and perspectives, as well as potentially influence the editorial agenda. It is crucial to have a pluralistic media landscape that reflects the diversity of society to ensure a robust democracy.

Furthermore, there are concerns about the erosion of journalistic ethics and standards in some parts of the media industry. Sensationalism, bias, and clickbait headlines can undermine the credibility of journalism and erode public trust. Maintaining high ethical standards is essential for preserving the integrity of the Fourth Estate.

Moreover, governments sometimes attempt to control or manipulate the media to serve their own interests. Press freedom is a cornerstone of democracy, and any attempts to curtail it pose a threat to democratic principles. Journalists must be able to operate independently without fear of censorship or reprisals.

The Fourth Estate plays a crucial role in ensuring a healthy and functioning democracy. It's like having an extra set of eyes and ears to keep our leaders accountable and inform the public.

The Fourth Estate refers to the media, including newspapers, television, radio, and online platforms. It acts as a watchdog, monitoring the actions of the government, holding them accountable, and providing the public with information. It's like having a trusted friend who keeps you updated on what's happening in the world.

One of the key roles of the media is to provide citizens with accurate and reliable information. It's like having a reliable source that you can turn to for news and updates. In a democracy, an informed citizenry is crucial for making informed decisions and participating in the democratic process.

The media also acts as a bridge between the government and the people. It's like being the messenger who delivers important information from the government to the public. Through investigative journalism and reporting, the media helps to uncover corruption, expose wrongdoing, and bring important issues to light.

In addition to providing information, the media also plays a vital role in shaping public opinion. It's like having a friend who shares their thoughts and perspectives on various issues. Through editorials, opinion pieces, and analysis, the media helps to shape public discourse and influence public opinion.

Furthermore, the media serves as a platform for diverse voices and opinions. It's like attending a party where everyone's ideas and perspectives are valued. In a democracy, it's important to have a range of viewpoints represented in the media to ensure a pluralistic and inclusive public sphere.

However, it's important to recognize that the media is not infallible. It can be influenced by various factors such as political bias, corporate interests, and sensationalism. It's like having a friend who sometimes gets caught up in gossip or exaggerates stories. This highlights the need for media literacy and critical thinking among citizens to discern credible information from misinformation or propaganda.

Moreover, the rise of social media has transformed the media landscape. It's like attending a party where everyone has a voice and can share their opinions instantly. While social media has provided a platform for citizen journalism and grassroots movements, it has also posed challenges in terms of misinformation, echo chambers, and the spread of fake news.

In a democratic society, a free and independent media is crucial. It's like having a friend who is unbiased and impartial. Journalists should have the freedom to investigate, report, and express.

Lastly, the financial sustainability of journalism poses a significant challenge in today's digital age. Traditional revenue models have been disrupted by online platforms, leading to job losses and reduced resources for investigative reporting. Finding sustainable business models that support quality journalism is crucial for maintaining a strong Fourth Estate.

In conclusion, the Fourth Estate plays a vital role in democracy by informing citizens, holding power accountable, fostering dialogue, and facilitating public participation. However, it faces challenges such as misinformation, concentration of ownership, erosion of ethics, government control, and financial sustainability.

Chapter 8: Challenges to Democracy: Corruption and Power Concentration

Now let's dive into the challenges that democracy faces when it comes to corruption and power concentration. These are indeed significant issues that can undermine the very foundations of a democratic system.

Corruption is like a pesky bug that can eat away at the core of democracy. When public officials or those in positions of power abuse their authority for personal gain, it erodes the trust and confidence that citizens have in their government. Corruption can take various forms, such as bribery, embezzlement, or nepotism, and it can have severe consequences for the functioning of a democratic society.

When corruption runs rampant, it creates a distorted playing field where the interests of a few are prioritized over the needs of the many. It's like having a friend who always gets their way by bending the rules. This concentration of power in the hands of the corrupt can lead to unequal distribution of resources, limited access to public services, and a sense of injustice among the citizens.

Addressing the challenges of corruption and power concentration requires a multi-faceted approach. Firstly, strengthening institutions and promoting transparency and accountability are crucial. This includes implementing effective anti-corruption measures, such as robust legal frameworks, independent oversight bodies, and whistleblower protection. Additionally, promoting transparency in campaign financing and lobbying can help reduce the influence of money in politics.

Secondly, promoting civic participation and empowering citizens is essential to counter power concentration. This can be achieved through initiatives such as citizen education programs, grassroots movements, and strengthening civil society organizations. By empowering citizens to actively engage in political processes, it helps to ensure that power is distributed more evenly and that decision-making reflects the interests of the broader population.

Furthermore, fostering a culture of integrity and ethical leadership is vital in combating corruption and preventing power concentration. This involves promoting ethical behavior among public officials through training programs, codes of conduct, and enforcement mechanisms. Additionally, promoting a free press and protecting journalists' rights can help expose corruption and hold those in power accountable.

Power concentration is another challenge that democracy faces. When power becomes concentrated in the hands of a few individuals or groups, it can lead to the marginalization of certain voices and perspectives. It's like attending a party where only a select few get to make all the decisions. This concentration of power can hinder the democratic principle of equal representation and limit the ability of citizens to participate in the decision-making process.

To ensure a healthy democracy, power needs to be distributed and shared among various institutions and actors. It's like having a party where everyone gets a chance to contribute and have their voices heard. Separation of powers, checks and balances, and free and fair elections are essential mechanisms to prevent power concentration and promote democratic governance.

Furthermore, media freedom and an independent judiciary are crucial in holding those in power accountable. It's like having a friend who keeps you in check and reminds you of your responsibilities. A vibrant civil society, including NGOs and grassroots movements, also plays a vital role in challenging power concentration and advocating for the rights and interests of the marginalized.

However, addressing these challenges is not a one-time fix. It requires ongoing efforts, vigilance, and active citizen engagement.

Challenges to Democracy: Corruption and Power Concentration

Democracy is a system of government that is based on the principles of equality, freedom, and the participation of citizens in decision-making processes. However, despite its many advantages, democracy faces several challenges that threaten its very foundation. Two significant challenges to democracy are corruption and power concentration.

Corruption is a pervasive problem in many democratic societies. It refers to the misuse of public office for personal gain or the abuse of power for private interests. Corruption undermines the principles of transparency, accountability, and fairness that are essential for a functioning democracy. When public officials engage in corrupt practices such as bribery, embezzlement, or nepotism, it erodes trust in government institutions and leads to a loss of faith in the democratic system.

Corruption poses a significant challenge to democracy because it distorts the allocation of resources and undermines economic development. When public funds are siphoned off through corrupt practices, it deprives citizens of essential services such as healthcare, education, and infrastructure. Moreover, corruption creates an uneven playing field for businesses, as those who engage in corrupt practices gain unfair advantages over their competitors. This not only hampers economic growth but also perpetuates inequality within society.

Another challenge to democracy is power concentration. Power concentration occurs when a few individuals or groups hold disproportionate control over political and economic resources. This can take various forms, such as monopolies in industries or political dynasties that dominate the political landscape. When power is concentrated in the hands of a few, it limits the ability of ordinary citizens to participate meaningfully in decision-making processes.

Power concentration poses a threat to democracy because it leads to an imbalance of power and can result in authoritarian tendencies. When power is concentrated in the hands of a few individuals or groups, they can manipulate institutions and laws to serve their own interests rather than those of the broader population. This undermines the principles of equality and fairness that are fundamental to democracy.

Furthermore, power concentration can lead to the erosion of checks and balances within a democratic system. When power is concentrated, there is a higher likelihood of corruption and abuse of power. This can result in a lack of accountability and transparency, as those in power are less likely to be held responsible for their actions. In extreme cases, power concentration can lead to the emergence of authoritarian regimes that suppress dissent and curtail civil liberties.

In conclusion, corruption and power concentration pose significant challenges to democracy. These challenges undermine the principles of equality, fairness, transparency, and accountability that are essential for a functioning democratic system. Addressing these challenges requires a comprehensive approach that includes strengthening institutions, promoting civic participation, fostering integrity, and protecting freedom of the press.

Chapter 9: Human Rights and Democracy

Human rights and democracy are two interconnected concepts that form the foundation of a just and equitable society. Human rights refer to the basic rights and freedoms that every individual is entitled to, regardless of their race, gender, religion, or social status. These rights include the right to life, liberty, equality, and freedom of expression, among others. Democracy, on the other hand, is a system of government in which power is vested in the people, who exercise it either directly or through elected representatives.

Human rights and democracy go hand in hand because democracy provides the necessary framework for protecting and promoting human rights. In a democratic society, individuals have the right to participate in decision-making processes that affect their lives. They can vote for their representatives, express their opinions freely, and hold those in power accountable for their actions. This ensures that human rights are respected and upheld by the government.

Democracy also creates an environment conducive to the realization of human rights. It allows for the establishment of independent institutions such as courts and ombudsman offices that can protect individuals from abuses of power. It promotes transparency and accountability in governance, making it more difficult for violations of human rights to go unnoticed or unpunished.

Furthermore, democracy fosters inclusivity and diversity by ensuring equal opportunities for all members of society to participate in political processes. It guarantees minority rights and protects marginalized groups from discrimination. In a democratic society, everyone has a voice and is treated with dignity and respect.

However, it is important to note that democracy alone is not sufficient for the protection of human rights. A democratic system can still be flawed if it does not have strong institutions or if there is a lack of checks and balances on power. Therefore, it is crucial to have an independent judiciary, a free press, and civil society organizations that can monitor the government's actions and advocate for human rights.

Moreover, democracy should not be seen as a one-size-fits-all model. Different countries and cultures may have different interpretations of democracy, and it is important to respect their unique contexts and traditions. However, there are certain universal principles that should be upheld in any democratic society, such as the rule of law, respect for human rights, and the protection of minority rights.

In recent years, there has been a growing concern about the erosion of human rights and democracy in many parts of the world. Authoritarian regimes have cracked down on dissent, curtailed freedom of expression, and violated the rights of their citizens. This poses a threat not only to the individuals directly affected but also to the global community as a whole.

To address these challenges, it is crucial for governments, civil society organizations, and international institutions to work together to promote and protect human rights and democracy. This can be done through diplomatic pressure, economic sanctions, and support for local activists and organizations fighting for human rights.

Furthermore, education plays a vital role in promoting human rights and democracy. By raising awareness about these issues and teaching people about their rights and responsibilities as citizens, we can empower individuals to stand up for their own rights and advocate for positive change in their communiti

Human rights and democracy are essential pillars of a just and equitable society. They are interconnected concepts that reinforce each other.

Democracy provides the framework for protecting and promoting human rights, while human rights ensure that democracy is inclusive, transparent, and accountable. It is crucial for governments, civil society organizations, and individuals to work together to uphold these principles and create a world where everyone can enjoy their fundamental freedoms.

Human rights and democracy are intertwined concepts that form the bedrock of a just and inclusive society. Both are essential for the protection and promotion of individual freedoms, equality, and dignity. Let's explore this topic in depth.

1. Human rights are the basic rights and freedoms to which all individuals are entitled, regardless of their nationality, race, gender, or any other characteristic. These rights include civil, political, economic, social, and cultural rights. They encompass the right to life, liberty, equality, freedom of expression, and many more.

2. Democracy, on the other hand, is a system of government in which power rests with the people, who exercise their power directly or through elected

representatives. It ensures that citizens have the right to participate in decision-making processes and have a say in shaping the policies that affect their lives.

3. Human rights and democracy are closely connected because democracy provides the framework for the protection and realization of human rights. It establishes the rule of law, protects individual freedoms, and guarantees equal rights and opportunities for all citizens.

4. In a democratic society, human rights are not just legal protections but also the guiding principles that shape policies and laws. They provide a moral compass for governments and individuals, ensuring that the rights and dignity of every person are respected and upheld.

5. Democracy without respect for human rights can become a hollow shell, as it may fail to address the needs and aspirations of all members of society. Conversely, human rights without a democratic framework can lack the mechanisms necessary for their enforcement and protection.

6. Human rights are the foundation of a functioning democracy. They enable individuals to participate in the political process, express their opinions, and hold their governments accountable. Without human rights, democracy can become an empty exercise, devoid of substance and meaning.

7. Democracy provides the space and opportunity for marginalized groups to have their voices heard and their rights protected. It ensures that no one is left behind or excluded from the decision-making process. It's like attending a party where everyone gets a chance to contribute and have their voices heard.

8. Human rights and democracy also foster social cohesion and inclusivity. By guaranteeing equal rights and opportunities for all, they promote a sense of belonging and unity among diverse individuals and communities. It's like having a party where everyone feels welcome and valued.

9. Furthermore, human rights and democracy are essential for sustainable development. They create an enabling environment for economic growth, social progress, and environmental sustainability. It's like having a friend who supports your dreams and helps you achieve your goals.

Chapter 10: Democracy and Globalization

Democracy and globalization are two interconnected concepts that have a significant impact on the world today. Democracy refers to a system of government where power is vested in the people, who exercise it either directly or through elected representatives. Globalization, on the other hand, refers to the increasing interconnectedness and interdependence of countries through the exchange of goods, services, information, and ideas.

Democracy and globalization have both positive and negative implications for each other. On one hand, democracy can be seen as a facilitator of globalization. Democracies tend to have more open economies and societies, which encourages trade, investment, and cultural exchange between nations. This openness promotes economic growth and development, as well as the spread of democratic values and human rights.

Globalization also has the potential to strengthen democracy by exposing citizens to different ideas and perspectives from around the world. The free flow of information through technology and media platforms allows people to access diverse viewpoints and challenge their own beliefs. This can lead to a more informed citizenry and a greater demand for transparency, accountability, and participation in governance.

However, globalization can also pose challenges to democracy. As economies become more integrated, multinational corporations gain significant influence over national policies. This can undermine democratic decision-making processes as corporate interests may take precedence over public welfare. Moreover, globalization can exacerbate inequalities within and between countries, leading to social unrest and political instability.

Furthermore, globalization can also weaken national sovereignty by limiting the ability of governments to regulate their own economies or protect their citizens from global forces. International organizations such as the World Trade Organization (WTO) or International Monetary Fund (IMF) often impose conditions on countries in exchange for financial assistance or market access. These conditions may not always align with the preferences or needs of local populations.

Globalization has expanded the flow of information, enabling citizens in democratic societies to access diverse perspectives and ideas from around the world. This access to information enhances their ability to make informed decisions and engage in democratic processes.

Similarly, democracy can help shape the course of globalization. In democratic societies, citizens have the power to influence policies and regulations that govern international trade, finance, and other aspects of globalization. This ensures that the benefits and costs of globalization are distributed equitably and that the interests of all citizens are taken into account.

Globalization has also presented challenges to democratic governance. As countries become more interconnected, decisions made by international organizations, multinational corporations, and global financial institutions can impact the sovereignty of individual nations. This can sometimes limit the ability of democratic governments to respond to the needs and aspirations of their citizens.

However, globalization can also provide opportunities for democratic participation. It has facilitated the growth of civil society organizations, non-governmental organizations, and grassroots movements that advocate for human rights, environmental sustainability, and social justice on a global scale. These groups can leverage the interconnectedness of the world to amplify their voices and effect change.

Moreover, globalization has brought economic growth and development to many parts of the world. This economic progress can create a more favorable environment for the establishment and consolidation of democratic institutions. As people's living standards improve, they often demand more political freedoms and rights.

At the same time, the spread of democracy can contribute to a more stable and inclusive form of globalization. Democratic societies tend to prioritize human rights, labor standards, and environmental protection, which can lead to a more sustainable and equitable form of global integration.

In recent years, there has been a growing backlash against globalization in some democratic societies. This backlash is fueled by concerns about job losses due to outsourcing or automation, cultural homogenization, and the erosion of national identity. These sentiments have led to the rise of populist movements that advocate for protectionist policies and a more inward-looking approach to governance.

To address these challenges, it is crucial to ensure that globalization is inclusive and benefits all segments of society. Governments need to implement policies that promote equitable economic growth, protect workers' rights, and safeguard the environment. They should also strive to enhance democratic institutions and practices at both national and international levels.

In conclusion, democracy and globalization are intertwined phenomena that have complex interactions. While democracy can foster globalization by promoting openness and participation, globalization can both strengthen and undermine democracy. It is essential for governments, civil society organizations, and international institutions to work together to ensure that globalization is compatible with democratic values and serves the interests of all people.

VOTe
choice

Chapter 11: Democratic Institutions: Separation of Powers

Democratic institutions are a fundamental aspect of any democratic society. They serve as the framework for the functioning of a government and ensure that power is distributed and balanced among different branches. One of the key principles underlying democratic institutions is the separation of powers, which refers to the division of government responsibilities into distinct branches: the executive, legislative, and judicial.

The separation of powers is designed to prevent the concentration of power in any one branch and to provide checks and balances on each other. The executive branch, typically headed by a president or prime minister, is responsible for implementing and enforcing laws. The legislative branch, usually composed of a parliament or congress, is responsible for making laws. The judicial branch, consisting of courts and judges, interprets laws and ensures their constitutionality.

This division of powers ensures that no single branch becomes too powerful or dominant. It allows for a system of checks and balances where each branch can monitor and limit the actions of the others. For example, the legislative branch can pass laws that restrict the powers of the executive branch or impeach a president for misconduct. The judicial branch can declare laws or executive actions unconstitutional.

By separating powers, democratic institutions also promote accountability and transparency. Each branch has its own specific roles and responsibilities, which makes it easier to hold them accountable for their actions. For instance, if the executive branch abuses its power or violates the law, it can be held accountable through impeachment or legal challenges in court.

Furthermore, separation of powers helps to protect individual rights and liberties. The judiciary acts as a safeguard against potential abuses by the other branches. It ensures that laws are applied fairly and consistently, protects individuals from unjust treatment by the government, and upholds constitutional rights.

Another important aspect of separation of powers is that it encourages cooperation and compromise among different branches. In order to pass legislation or implement policies effectively, there needs to be collaboration between the executive and legislative branches. This promotes dialogue and negotiation, leading to more inclusive and representative decision-making processes.

Moreover, separation of powers fosters stability and continuity in democratic systems. It prevents sudden shifts in power and provides a system of checks and balances that helps to maintain political equilibrium. This stability is crucial for the functioning of democratic institutions and the overall governance of a country.

However, it is important to note that the separation of powers is not always perfect or absolute. There can be overlaps and interactions between branches, especially in practice. For example, the executive branch may have some influence over the legislative process through veto powers or proposing legislation. Similarly, the judiciary may be influenced by political considerations or appointments made by the executive branch.

In addition, maintaining a balance between the branches can sometimes be challenging. One branch may become too dominant or attempt to undermine the powers of others. This can lead to power struggles and conflicts within democratic institutions.

Overall, while the separation of powers is an essential principle of democratic institutions, it requires constant vigilance and commitment to ensure its effectiveness. It serves as a crucial safeguard against abuses of power, promotes accountability and transparency, protects individual rights, encourages cooperation among branches, and fosters stability in democratic systems.

The separation of powers is a fundamental principle of democratic institutions that ensures a system of checks and balances, preventing the concentration of power in any one branch of government. Let's explore this concept in more detail.

In a democratic system, the separation of powers refers to the division of government into three distinct branches: the executive, the legislative, and the judicial. Each branch has specific responsibilities and powers, which act as a safeguard against tyranny and abuse of power.

The executive branch, headed by the president or prime minister, is responsible for implementing and enforcing laws. It is tasked with executing policies, managing the day-to-day affairs of the government, and representing the country on the international stage.

The legislative branch, which consists of the parliament or congress, is responsible for making laws. It represents the interests of the people and serves as a forum for debate, discussion, and decision-making. The legislative branch also has the power to oversee and scrutinize the actions of the executive branch.

The judicial branch, which includes the courts and judges, is responsible for interpreting and applying the law. It ensures that laws are enforced fairly and impartially, and it acts as a check on the other branches of government. The judiciary has the power to review the constitutionality of laws and to resolve disputes between individuals or between the government and its citizens.

The separation of powers is crucial because it prevents any one branch from becoming too powerful or dominating the others. This system of checks and balances ensures that no single individual or group can abuse their authority or violate the rights of the people.

For example, the executive branch may propose and enforce laws, but it is the legislative branch that ultimately approves or rejects them. This ensures that laws are subject to scrutiny and debate, and that they reflect the will of the people.

Similarly, the judicial branch acts as a check on both the executive and legislative branches. It has the power to declare laws or actions unconstitutional, ensuring that the rights of individuals are protected and that the government operates within the bounds of the law.

The separation of powers also fosters accountability and transparency in government. Each branch is accountable to the people and must answer for its actions. This accountability is essential for maintaining public trust and confidence in democratic institutions.

However, it is important to note that the separation of powers does not mean that the branches operate in complete isolation.

Chapter 12: Federalism and Democracy

Federalism and democracy are two fundamental principles of governance that play a crucial role in shaping the political systems of many countries around the world. While they are distinct concepts, they often go hand in hand, as federalism provides a framework for the practice of democracy.

Federalism is a system of government in which power is divided between a central authority and regional or state governments. It is based on the principle of decentralization, where different levels of government have their own spheres of influence and autonomy. This division of power helps to prevent the concentration of authority in one entity, ensuring a more balanced distribution of power.

One key advantage of federalism is that it allows for the accommodation of diverse interests within a country. Different regions or states may have unique cultural, linguistic, or economic characteristics, and federalism provides them with the opportunity to govern themselves according to their specific needs and preferences. This promotes local autonomy and allows for greater representation and participation at the regional level.

Furthermore, federalism fosters competition among regions or states, leading to innovation and efficiency in governance. When different regions have the power to make their own decisions and implement policies tailored to their specific circumstances, it encourages experimentation and learning from each other's successes and failures. This can lead to more effective governance practices overall.

In addition to promoting diversity and competition, federalism also serves as a check on central authority. By dividing power between different levels of government, it helps prevent abuses of power and tyranny. The existence of multiple centers of authority ensures that no single entity can dominate the entire political system, protecting individual rights and liberties.

Democracy, on the other hand, is a system of government in which power resides with the people. It is characterized by free and fair elections, where citizens have the right to choose their representatives through popular vote.

Democracy emphasizes principles such as equality, participation, accountability, and transparency.

Democracy complements federalism by providing a mechanism for the people to express their preferences and hold their elected representatives accountable. Through regular elections, citizens have the opportunity to voice their opinions and shape the direction of government policies. This ensures that power remains in the hands of the people and prevents the concentration of authority in a few individuals or groups.

Moreover, democracy promotes inclusivity and protects minority rights. In a democratic system, all citizens have equal rights and opportunities to participate in political processes. This includes the right to vote, freedom of speech, assembly, and association. These democratic principles are essential for safeguarding the interests of minority groups and preventing discrimination or marginalization.

Federalism is a system of government in which power is divided and shared between a central authority and regional or state governments. This distribution of power allows for a balance between national unity and regional autonomy. In a federal system, the central government holds authority over matters of national importance, such as defense, foreign policy, and currency. On the other hand, regional or state governments have the power to govern and make decisions on local issues, such as education, healthcare, and transportation.

Federalism promotes democracy by providing opportunities for citizen participation and representation at multiple levels of government. It allows for diverse perspectives and local preferences to be taken into account in decision-making processes. The division of power in a federal system helps prevent the concentration of power in a single authority, reducing the risk of tyranny and promoting the protection of individual rights and liberties.

Federalism also fosters political stability and unity in diverse countries. It allows for different regions with distinct cultures, languages, and histories to have a degree of self-governance while remaining part of a larger political entity.

Through federalism, citizens have the opportunity to engage in politics and participate in decision-making processes at both the national and regional levels. This enhances democratic values such as civic engagement, representation, and accountability.

Federalism encourages competition and experimentation among different regions or states. It allows for the implementation of different policies and approaches to address local needs and challenges. This enables the sharing of best practices and the development of innovative solutions to common problems.

By providing a system of checks and balances, federalism helps prevent the abuse of power and promotes accountability. The central government and regional governments can serve as checks on each other, ensuring that decisions are made in the best interest of the people.

However, federalism can also present challenges in terms of coordination and cooperation between different levels of government. It requires effective communication and collaboration to address issues that span across regions, such as economic disparities or environmental concerns.

In a democratic federal system, citizens have the opportunity to vote and elect representatives at both the national and regional levels. This ensures that their voices are heard and that decisions are made in accordance with their preferences and interests. Federalism allows for the protection of minority rights and interests. Regional or state governments can serve as a safeguard against the dominance of the majority.

Federalism enhances democracy by providing a framework for decentralized decision-making and representation. It allows for a more diverse range of voices to be heard at different levels of government, ensuring that regional interests are adequately represented in the political process. This helps prevent the dominance of majority interests over minority concerns.

Furthermore, federalism can help mitigate social and political conflicts within a country. By granting regions or states greater autonomy, it allows for the peaceful resolution of disputes between different groups with distinct identities or interests. Rather than resorting to violence or secessionist movements, federalism provides a platform for negotiation and compromise.

However, federalism and democracy also face challenges that need to be addressed for their effective implementation. One challenge is striking the right balance between central authority and regional autonomy. While decentralization is important for promoting local governance and representation, there is also a need for coordination and cooperation among different levels of government to address national issues effectively.

Another challenge is ensuring that democratic processes are inclusive and participatory. While elections are an essential component of democracy, they should be free from manipulation or exclusionary practices.

Chapter 13: Democracy and Social Movements

Democracy and social movements are deeply interconnected, as both play a crucial role in shaping societies and advocating for change. Democracy provides the framework for citizens to express their opinions, participate in decision-making processes, and hold their governments accountable. Social movements, on the other hand, are collective efforts by groups of individuals who share common goals and values to bring about social, political, or cultural change.

One of the fundamental principles of democracy is the right to freedom of expression and assembly. This allows individuals to voice their concerns and grievances through peaceful protests, demonstrations, and other forms of activism. Social movements often emerge when people feel that their voices are not being heard within the existing political system. They mobilize to challenge injustices, advocate for marginalized groups, and demand reforms.

Social movements have played a significant role in advancing democracy throughout history. From the civil rights movement in the United States to the anti-apartheid movement in South Africa, these movements have fought against discrimination, inequality, and oppressive regimes. They have pushed for legal reforms, constitutional changes, and the protection of human rights.

Furthermore, social movements contribute to democratic consolidation by fostering civic engagement and political participation. They encourage citizens to become active members of society by raising awareness about important issues and mobilizing people to take action. By doing so, they strengthen democratic institutions and promote a more inclusive and participatory democracy.

Social movements also serve as a check on power within democracies. They act as watchdogs by monitoring government actions, exposing corruption or abuses of power, and demanding transparency and accountability. Through their activism, they ensure that elected officials remain responsive to the needs and demands of the people they represent.

However, social movements can also face challenges within democratic systems. Governments may attempt to suppress or undermine these movements through various means such as restrictive laws, surveillance, or even violence. In some cases, social movements may be labeled as threats to national security or portrayed as radical or extremist groups. These challenges highlight the importance of protecting civil liberties and ensuring that democratic systems provide space for dissent and peaceful protest.

Democracy is a system of government where power rests with the people, who exercise their authority through voting and participation in decision-making processes. Social movements, on the other hand, are collective efforts by a group of individuals who come together to advocate for social, political, or cultural change.

Democracy provides a platform for social movements to thrive by guaranteeing freedom of speech, assembly, and association. It allows individuals to express their grievances, mobilize support, and demand change through peaceful means. Social movements often emerge in response to perceived injustices, inequality, or the violation of human rights. They seek to address these issues by raising awareness, organizing protests or demonstrations, and advocating for policy reforms.

Democracy provides a framework for social movements to engage with the political system. Movements can influence public opinion, shape the political agenda, and hold elected officials accountable through various channels such as lobbying, advocacy, and grassroots organizing. Social movements play a crucial role in expanding and deepening democracy. They challenge the status quo, promote inclusivity, and push for the recognition and protection of the rights of marginalized groups, such as women, racial and ethnic minorities, LGBTQ+ individuals, and indigenous communities.

Social movements act as a catalyst for social change by challenging societal norms, promoting progressive values, and driving policy reforms. They have been instrumental in advancing civil rights, labor rights, environmental protection, gender equality, and other social justice causes.

In a democratic society, social movements contribute to the pluralistic nature of public discourse. They bring diverse perspectives, amplify marginalized voices, and foster dialogue on critical issues, thereby enriching the democratic process.

Democracy provides social movements with avenues for participation and influence within the political system. Movements can form alliances with political parties, engage in electoral campaigns, and even transition into formal political organizations to enact change from within. Social movements can also act as a check on the government and other institutions by holding them accountable for their actions and policies. Through peaceful protests, civil disobedience, and advocacy, movements can expose corruption, challenge oppressive policies, and demand transparency and accountability.

However, the relationship between democracy and social movements is not without challenges. Movements may face repression, censorship, or even violence from governments or powerful interests

Moreover, social movements can sometimes face internal divisions and conflicts. Different groups within a movement may have divergent goals or strategies, leading to tensions and disagreements. However, these differences can also be seen as a strength, as they allow for a diversity of perspectives and approaches to addressing social issues.

In recent years, social media and digital technologies have significantly impacted social movements and democracy. Online platforms have provided new avenues for organizing, mobilizing, and spreading awareness about social causes. They have facilitated the rapid dissemination of information, allowing movements to reach a wider audience and gain support both nationally and internationally.

However, the rise of social media has also brought challenges. The spread of misinformation or fake news can undermine the credibility of social movements and distort public discourse. Additionally, online platforms can be used by governments or powerful interests to manipulate public opinion or suppress dissent.

In conclusion, democracy and social movements are deeply intertwined. Social movements are essential for democratic societies as they advocate for change, challenge injustices, promote civic engagement, and hold governments accountable. They contribute to democratic consolidation by fostering participation and inclusivity. However, they also face challenges within democratic systems, such as government repression or internal divisions. The advent of digital technologies has further shaped the landscape of social movements and democracy, providing new opportunities but also posing new risks. Overall, the relationship between democracy and social movements is dynamic and complex, with both influencing each other in significant ways.

Chapter 14: Democracy and the Economy

Democracy and the economy are two interconnected aspects of society that have a significant impact on each other. Democracy refers to a system of government where power is vested in the people, allowing them to participate in decision-making processes through voting and representation. On the other hand, the economy encompasses the production, distribution, and consumption of goods and services within a society.

One of the fundamental principles of democracy is the protection of individual rights and freedoms. This includes economic rights such as property ownership, entrepreneurship, and fair competition. A democratic system ensures that individuals have the freedom to engage in economic activities without undue interference from the government or other powerful entities. This creates an environment conducive to economic growth and innovation.

Democracy also promotes accountability and transparency in economic governance. Through mechanisms such as free press, independent judiciary, and checks and balances, democratic societies can hold their leaders accountable for their economic decisions. This helps prevent corruption, favoritism, and misuse of public resources, fostering a more efficient allocation of resources within the economy.

Furthermore, democracy encourages inclusivity and equal opportunities in economic participation. By giving every citizen a voice in decision-making processes, democratic systems aim to reduce social inequalities and promote social mobility. This allows individuals from all backgrounds to contribute to and benefit from economic development.

In terms of economic performance, democracies have shown a tendency towards stability and long-term growth. The open exchange of ideas, free flow of information, and respect for property rights create an environment that attracts investment and fosters entrepreneurship. Moreover, democratic institutions tend to promote sound economic policies that prioritize sustainable development over short-term gains.

However, it is important to note that democracy alone does not guarantee economic success. The specific policies implemented by governments play a crucial role in shaping the economy. For instance, countries with strong institutions that protect property rights, enforce contracts, provide infrastructure, invest in education and healthcare tend to experience higher levels of economic development.

Additionally, democracy can face challenges in managing economic issues such as income inequality, unemployment, and poverty. The democratic process often involves diverse interests and opinions, making it difficult to reach consensus on economic policies. This can lead to policy gridlock or short-term decision-making that may not address long-term economic challenges effectively.

Moreover, democratic systems are susceptible to political pressures and populism, which can influence economic decision-making. Politicians may prioritize short-term popularity over long-term economic stability, leading to unsustainable policies or excessive government spending. This can result in inflation, fiscal deficits, and debt accumulation, which negatively impact the economy.

Furthermore, democracy can also face challenges from powerful interest groups that seek to influence economic policies for their own benefit. These groups may lobby for regulations that protect their market dominance or seek preferential treatment from the government. Such rent-seeking behavior can distort market competition and hinder economic growth.

In conclusion, democracy and the economy are deeply intertwined. Democracy provides a framework for protecting individual rights, promoting accountability, inclusivity, and equal opportunities in economic participation. It also fosters stability, innovation, and long-term growth. However, democracy alone is not sufficient for economic success; effective governance and sound economic policies are equally important. Challenges such as income inequality, policy gridlock, populism, and rent-seeking behavior must be addressed to ensure that democracy and the economy work hand in hand for the betterment of society.

Democracy and the economy are intricately linked, and understanding their relationship is crucial in comprehending the dynamics of modern societies. Here are some key points to consider:

1. Democracy provides a framework that allows for economic freedom and entrepreneurship. It enables individuals to start businesses, invest in various sectors, and pursue economic opportunities without undue interference from the state.

2. In a democratic society, economic policies are shaped through public deliberation and participation. The government's economic decisions, such as taxation, regulation, and public spending, are subject to scrutiny and debate, ensuring a more inclusive and accountable economic system.

3. Democracy promotes a fair and level playing field in the economy by advocating for equal rights, access to resources, and opportunities for all citizens. It helps to prevent economic monopolies, promote competition, and reduce income inequality.

4. Through democratic processes, citizens have the power to influence economic policies and shape the priorities of the government. They can vote for representatives who align with their economic interests and hold them accountable for their actions and decisions.

5. Democracy encourages transparency and accountability in economic governance. It promotes the rule of law, protects property rights, and ensures that economic institutions operate in a fair and equitable manner.

6. In a democratic society, the government has a responsibility to provide social safety nets and address economic disparities. Through policies such as progressive taxation, welfare programs, and public services, democracy aims to reduce poverty, promote social mobility, and create a more equitable distribution of wealth.

7. Democracy fosters innovation and economic growth by fostering an environment that encourages creativity, critical thinking, and diversity of ideas. It allows for the free flow of information, which is essential for entrepreneurship, technological advancements, and economic development.

8. A democratic system provides stability and predictability, which are crucial for attracting domestic and foreign investments. Investors are more likely to allocate capital to countries with a stable political environment, strong institutions, and respect for the rule of law.

9. Democracy promotes consumer protection and ensures that markets operate in the best interest of the public. Through regulatory frameworks, consumer rights are safeguarded, and mechanisms for fair competition and dispute resolution are established.

10. Economic policies in a democratic society are more likely to be responsive to the needs and aspirations of the people. The government is accountable to its citizens, and their feedback and demands shape economic decision-making processes.

11. Democracy encourages economic resilience by fostering a diverse and inclusive economy. It supports sectors such as small and medium scale enterprises.

Chapter 15: Democracy in Practice: Case Studies

Here are some relevant case studies of democracy

Case Study: United States

The United States is often considered a prime example of democracy in practice. With its system of checks and balances, separation of powers, and regular elections, the country has established a strong democratic tradition. However, it is not without its flaws. The influence of money in politics, gerrymandering, and voter suppression are some of the challenges that the US faces in ensuring a truly representative democracy.

Case Study: India

India is the world's largest democracy, with a diverse population and a federal system of government. Despite its size and complexity, India has managed to hold regular elections since gaining independence in 1947. However, issues such as corruption, caste-based politics, and religious tensions pose significant challenges to the practice of democracy in the country.

Case Study: South Africa

South Africa's transition from apartheid to democracy is a remarkable case study. The country held its first non-racial elections in 1994, marking the end of white minority rule. Since then, South Africa has made significant progress in building democratic institutions and promoting equality. However, challenges such as corruption, inequality, and social unrest continue to test the strength of its democracy.

YOUR VOICE
YOUR VOTE
VOTE

Case Study: Brazil

Brazil has experienced both successes and setbacks in its democratic journey. The country held free and fair elections after years of military dictatorship ended in 1985. However, political corruption scandals and economic crises have eroded public trust in democratic institutions. The rise of populist leaders also poses a threat to Brazil's democratic foundations.

Case Study: Germany

Germany's post-World War II transformation into a stable democracy is an inspiring case study. Through rigorous efforts to confront its Nazi past and establish democratic institutions, Germany has become one of Europe's leading democracies. However, recent challenges such as the rise of far-right movements highlight the ongoing need for vigilance in protecting democratic values.

Case Study: Japan

Japan's democratic journey began after World War II, with the adoption of a new constitution that enshrined democratic principles. The country has since built strong democratic institutions and held regular elections. However, issues such as political apathy among young people and the influence of vested interests in politics pose challenges to Japan's democracy.

Case Study: Australia

Australia is known for its robust democracy, characterized by compulsory voting, independent judiciary, and a vibrant civil society. However, recent debates over issues like immigration policy and indigenous rights have raised questions about the inclusivity and fairness of Australia's democracy.

Case Study: Canada

Canada is often cited as a model of liberal democracy, with its respect for human rights, multiculturalism, and peaceful transitions of power. However, challenges such as the representation of indigenous peoples and regional disparities highlight the need for ongoing efforts to strengthen democratic practices in the country.

Case Study: Norway
Norway consistently ranks high in global democracy indices due to its strong institutions, transparency, and high levels of citizen participation. The country's commitment to social welfare and equality also contributes to its successful democratic practice. However, debates over issues like immigration and climate change reveal ongoing tensions within Norwegian society.

Case Study: South Korea
South Korea's transition from military dictatorship to democracy in the late 20th century is a remarkable case study. Through mass protests and grassroots movements, South Koreans successfully fought for democratic reforms. However, challenges such as political polarization and corruption continue to test the strength of South Korea's democracy.

Other books from the publisher

https://mybook.to/Grow_your_mind
https://mybook.to/TravelAdventure
https://mybook.to/WinterApple
https://mybook.to/Teenage_Sexuality
https://mybook.to/love_language

Chapter 16: The Future of Democracy: Trends and Prospects

The future of democracy is a topic of great importance and speculation. As the world continues to evolve and face new challenges, it is crucial to analyze the trends and prospects for democracy in order to ensure its sustainability and effectiveness.

One trend that has emerged in recent years is the rise of populism. Populist leaders have gained popularity by appealing to the grievances and frustrations of the masses, often by using divisive rhetoric and promising quick solutions to complex problems. This trend poses a threat to democracy as it can undermine institutions, erode trust in democratic processes, and lead to the concentration of power in the hands of a few.

Another trend is the increasing influence of technology on democratic processes. The advent of social media and digital platforms has provided new avenues for citizen engagement, political activism, and information dissemination. However, it has also raised concerns about privacy, misinformation, and the manipulation of public opinion. As technology continues to advance, it will be essential to strike a balance between harnessing its potential for democratic participation while safeguarding against its negative impacts.

Furthermore, globalization has had both positive and negative effects on democracy. On one hand, globalization has facilitated the spread of democratic values, norms, and institutions across borders. It has also created opportunities for international cooperation and collaboration on issues such as human rights and climate change. On the other hand, globalization has also led to economic inequalities, which can undermine democratic principles by concentrating power in the hands of wealthy elites.

Demographic changes are another factor that will shape the future of democracy. The world is experiencing rapid urbanization, aging populations, and increasing diversity. These changes can have profound implications for political dynamics as different groups may have varying interests and priorities. Ensuring inclusivity and representation for all segments of society will be crucial for maintaining a vibrant and robust democracy.

The role of civil society organizations and non-governmental actors will also be instrumental in shaping the future of democracy. These organizations play a vital role in advocating for citizens' rights, monitoring government actions, and holding leaders accountable. Strengthening civil society and ensuring their independence and effectiveness will be essential for the continued functioning of democracy.

In terms of prospects, there are reasons to be both optimistic and cautious. On one hand, the desire for freedom, equality, and participation remains strong among people around the world. The spread of democratic ideals and aspirations is evident in movements such as the Arab Spring and pro-democracy protests in various countries. This indicates that there is a widespread demand for democratic governance.

However, there are also challenges that need to be addressed. The erosion of trust in democratic institutions, rising inequality, and the spread of disinformation pose significant threats to democracy. Additionally, the rise of authoritarian regimes in some parts of the world demonstrates that democracy is not guaranteed or irreversible.

To ensure a positive future for democracy, it will be crucial to address these challenges. This includes strengthening democratic institutions, promoting transparency and accountability, fostering inclusive political systems, and addressing economic inequalities. It will also require investing in education and media literacy to empower citizens to critically engage with information and participate meaningfully in democratic processes.

International cooperation will also play a vital role in shaping the future of democracy. Global challenges such as climate change, terrorism, and pandemics require collective action and coordination among nations. By working together, countries can promote democratic values and norms on a global scale while also learning from each other's experiences.

As we look ahead, there are several trends and prospects that can shape the path of democracy in the years to come. some of these trends and prospects are:

1. Technological Advancements: Technology continues to evolve at a rapid pace, and it has the potential to transform the way democracies function. From online voting systems to digital platforms for citizen engagement, technology can enhance accessibility, transparency, and participation in democratic processes.

2. Rise of Populism: Populist movements have gained traction in recent years, challenging traditional democratic norms and institutions. The future of democracy will depend on how societies navigate the complexities of

populism while upholding democratic values such as inclusivity, tolerance, and respect for diversity.

3. Globalization and Interconnectedness: In an increasingly interconnected world, the future of democracy will be influenced by global challenges that require international cooperation. Issues like climate change, migration, and economic inequality will demand collaborative efforts and cross-border solutions.

4. Youth Engagement: The involvement of young people in democratic processes will shape the future of democracy. With their unique perspectives and aspirations, young voices can drive change, push for social justice, and bring fresh ideas to the table.

5. Democratic Backsliding: While democracy has made significant progress in many parts of the world, there are concerns about democratic backsliding in certain regions. The future of democracy will depend on efforts to safeguard democratic institutions, protect human rights, and promote democratic values globally.

6. Social Media and Disinformation: The rise of social media has revolutionized communication and information sharing. However, it has also presented challenges such as the spread of disinformation and the manipulation of public opinion. Addressing these challenges will be crucial for the future of democracy.

7. Climate Crisis and Sustainability: The future of democracy will be intertwined with the urgent need to address the climate crisis and promote sustainable development. Democratic societies will need to prioritize environmental stewardship, integrate climate policies, and engage citizens in shaping sustainable futures.

8. Gender Equality and Diversity: The future of democracy will be shaped by efforts to achieve gender equality and promote diversity and inclusion. Ensuring equal representation and participation of women, ethnic minorities, and marginalized groups will be essential for a thriving democracy.

9. Civic Education and Empowerment: Strengthening civic education and empowering citizens to actively participate in democratic processes will be

vital for the future of democracy. Educating individuals about their rights, responsibilities, and the importance of democratic values
In conclusion, the future of democracy is both promising and uncertain. While there are challenges to overcome, there are also opportunities to strengthen democratic governance and ensure its longevity. By understanding the trends and prospects for democracy, we can work towards building a more inclusive, transparent, and participatory political system that serves the needs and aspirations of all citizens.

Conclusion: The Vitality of Democracy

In conclusion, democracy is a vital system that promotes the well-being and progress of societies. It ensures that power is distributed among the people, allowing for a more inclusive and fair decision-making process. Democracy encourages citizen participation, fostering a sense of ownership and responsibility among individuals. It also provides a platform for diverse voices to be heard, leading to better representation and the protection of minority rights.

One of the key strengths of democracy is its ability to promote stability and prevent conflicts. By providing mechanisms for peaceful transfer of power, democracy reduces the likelihood of political violence and upheaval. Additionally, democratic societies tend to have stronger institutions and rule of law, which contribute to overall stability and economic development.

Furthermore, democracy encourages accountability and transparency in governance. Elected officials are answerable to the people they represent, creating a system where leaders are held responsible for their actions. This accountability helps combat corruption and abuse of power, as citizens have the power to vote out those who do not fulfill their promises or act in their best interests.

Democracy also fosters social cohesion by promoting dialogue and compromise. In a democratic society, different opinions and perspectives are valued, leading to constructive debates and negotiations. This allows for the resolution of conflicts through peaceful means, rather than resorting to violence or suppression.

Moreover, democracy empowers individuals by granting them fundamental rights and freedoms. Citizens have the right to express their opinions, assemble peacefully, and participate in decision-making processes. These rights create an environment where individuals can pursue their goals freely and without fear of repression.

Additionally, democracy encourages innovation and progress by allowing for the free exchange of ideas. In a democratic society, individuals are encouraged to think critically and challenge existing norms. This intellectual freedom leads to advancements in various fields such as science, technology, arts, and culture.

Furthermore, democracy promotes social justice by addressing inequalities and protecting vulnerable groups. Through democratic processes such as elections and policy-making, marginalized communities have the opportunity to voice their concerns and advocate for their rights. This ensures that the needs of all citizens are taken into account and that no one is left behind.

Moreover, democracy provides a platform for peaceful resolution of conflicts. By allowing different groups to participate in decision-making processes, democracy reduces the likelihood of violence as people can express their grievances through peaceful means. This contributes to long-term stability and social harmony.

Furthermore, democracy promotes international cooperation and peace. Democracies tend to have more peaceful relations with each other, as they share common values such as respect for human rights and rule of law. Democratic countries are also more likely to engage in diplomatic negotiations rather than resorting to military actions.

In conclusion, democracy is a vital system that ensures the well-being and progress of societies. It promotes stability, accountability, social cohesion, individual empowerment, innovation, social justice, conflict resolution, international cooperation, and peace. While no system is perfect, democracy provides a framework that allows for continuous improvement and adaptation to changing circumstances. It is essential for the protection of fundamental rights and freedoms and the advancement of societies towards a more inclusive and prosperous future.